T0036324

To my friend and mentor Valencia King Nelson, my beloved "VKN," who harnessed the power of the Internet and founded AfriGeneas, where this poem first appeared.
To my friend Mattie Brewer of Uvalde, Texas, who introduced me to the celebration of Juneteenth.—S. K. R.

For my mother, Evelyn Bostic, and my middle school art teacher, Ellen Kuenzel.
These women were the first to believe in me and my talent.
Thank you both for being my mother, teacher, and mentor.—A. B.

Union Square & Co., LLC, is a subsidiary of Sterling Publishing Co., Inc.

ISBN 978-1-4549-4374-7

For information about custom editions, special sales, and premium purchases, please contact specialsales@unionsquareandco.com.

Printed in the United States of America

Lot #:
2 4 6 8 10 9 7 5 3

08/22

unionsquareandco.com

Cover and interior design by Jo Obarowski

FREE AT LAST

A Juneteenth Poem

WRITTEN BY SOJOURNER KINCAID ROLLE   ILLUSTRATED BY ALEX BOSTIC

union
square
kids
NEW YORK

The news arrived in Galveston:

"THE WAR IS OVER!"

President Lincoln has decreed;
The Emancipation Proclamation declares:

"ALL WHO LIVE IN BONDAGE HERE SHALL FROM NOW UNTIL BE FREE."

After 300 years of forced bondage,
hands bound, descendants of Africa
picked up their souls—all that they owned—
leaving shackles where they fell on the ground,
headed for the nearest resting place to be found.

Some went no further than the shack out back;
oft only a shed—hard ground for a bed;
hard labor, no pay, but the will to survive.
’though they couldn’t call it their own,
they still declared, “This is my home.”

Some ran as far as they could go
into the service of the man
on the neighboring land.
Working for a pittance
and a little plot of space
much like they did when enslaved.

Some went to the nearest place of the Lord—
to some hollow place in the brush
or to a clearing in a grove
where folk gathered 'neath a still standing
tree and sang, "Thank you, Jesus, for delivering me."

Some made a beeline for the closest dance hall—
picking a tune, singing a song,
toasting the Union and Lady Luck,
settin' da flo, dancing the jig and the buck;
patting themselves on their whip-scarred backs;
reveling from night into day.

Some went the way of the river—
following the Rio Grande
or swimming the up-flowing Mississip.
Hastening to get as far as they could
thrusting their futures into sanctuary and unknown
friendless territory.

Some kept running like a stone on a hill—
never to grasp a firm place to rest.
Some even went to the promised land;
Wherever they went alone or abreast
at the end of their journey, they cried,
"I've done my best."

Every year in the Lone Star State, and
in towns from sea to sea,
sons and daughters of the ones who were held
—telling the stories that their families passed down—
celebrate the day their forebears could shout

"FREE AT LAST!
HALLELUJAH, I'M FREE!"

JUNETEENTH

They will always remember Juneteenth
the day their ancestors could sing
"FREE AT LAST!
HALLELUJAH, I'M FREE!"

AUTHOR'S NOTE

I came to the world of Juneteenth in the late 1980s when my friend Mrs. Mattie Brewer, from Texas, proposed that we organize a Juneteenth celebration for Santa Barbara. In preparing for that event, I researched the history and created a handout: "The Meaning of Juneteenth." Over the next few years, local groups would organize Juneteenth celebrations. Some years, Mattie would host a Juneteenth celebration at her home. Every year—whether in a community center or at a backyard barbeque—we marked the day.

During the early 1990s I met Yvette Sutton and Daisy Cotton, two residents of Oxnard, California, whose Texas roots sprang from the soil where Juneteenth originated. In 2004, my friend and mentor Mrs. Valencia King Nelson invited me to submit a poem for a special Juneteenth page that was being published by AfriGeneas, an online magazine. I wrote "Free at Last: A Juneteenth Poem" and sent it in.

Since then, my Juneteenth poem has been used by bloggers, community organizers, and educators all over the country and even in Canada. In 2018, a local group (now known as Healing Justice Santa Barbara) institutionalized our local Juneteenth celebrations. "Free at Last: A Juneteenth Poem" has been an integral part of subsequent celebrations.

Over the years, interest in my poem made me feel more connected than ever to the holiday. Recently I sensed a profound change. In the aftermath of George Floyd's murder, organizations like Black Lives Matter brought a heightened awareness to Juneteenth. That year, a Texas-based film company created a film based on a recording of me reading my poem aloud. The film was shared widely, and I received notes and comments from across the country and around the world, including Australia, Poland, Germany, South America, and the Caribbean.

One year later, 2021 held another change . . . the big surprise: Juneteenth was declared a national holiday! In the months before and since, there have been numerous critiques about the holiday's importance. One is that the Emancipation Proclamation, the executive order signed on January 1, 1863, did not end slavery in the United States, and many people remained in servitude even after June 19, 1865. It's true. Lincoln's executive order applied only to those who lived in the Confederate states. Slavery in the United States did not officially end until the Thirteenth Amendment to the Constitution was ratified on December 6, 1865.

Nevertheless, Juneteenth has emerged as the accepted date marking the end of slavery in the United States. It is a symbolic holiday, a representation of freedom for all who had been enslaved here.

Juneteenth commemorates a moment in time. That moment occurred in Texas for people who experienced the day and noted its importance. They and their descendants carried the memory of that moment forward, sharing it with future generations. In 1979, Texas became the first state to recognize Juneteenth as a holiday. Over the next fifty-two years, nearly all fifty states followed suit.

Now the poem emerges as a book for young people. A book that tells the world about this revered holiday. What it commemorates. What it celebrates. For me, it celebrates endurance, perseverance, resilience, and the joy of being alive.

Sojourner Kincaid Rolle
Santa Barbara, California